Chicks

battle the

Dudes™

Chicks
battle the
Dudes™

spinner/books™

San Francisco • Maastricht • Sydney

Warning: Small parts may be a choking hazard. Not for children under 3 years.

ACKNOWLEDGEMENTS

Special thanks to Suzanne Cracraft, Erin Davidson, Colin Dwyer, Lisa Fotenakes, Elise Gresch, Lynn Gustavson, Gareth Hopson, Vince Kurr, Joe Kwong, Cris Lehman, Maria Llull, Stefan Marti, Jeanette Miller, Bob Moog, Kristen Schoen, Ajay Yadav and Cherie Martorana.

Designers: Michelle Hill and Jeanette Miller

ISBN 1-57528-896-6

Printed in China

01 02 03 04 05 MP 9 8 7 6 5 4 3 2 1

CONTENTS

INTRODUCTION

Dear Friends,

Welcome to our newest Spinner Book, the books you can play™. *Chicks Battle the Dudes* is great fun for any gathering of men and women.

In putting this book together, I really tried to get inside the heads of my closest friends, both men and women. As you read and play, I hope that you learn some, but laugh lots. The questions in this book cover dozens of topics which generally interest one gender, but not both.

Enjoy playing *Chicks Battle the Dudes* with your regular gang or with new friends. Let me know which is the smarter sex in your circle.

Sincerely,

Bob

P.S. The chicks always win when I play!

RULES

Object

To be the first team to earn 15 points – and find out just how much you really know about the opposite sex!

Getting Started

First things first: grab a pen and paper to keep track of your points.

Next, divide into two teams – women on the Chicks team, men on the Dudes. The Chicks go first.

A member of the Dudes team flips to the beginning of the Chicks section and reads the first question to the Chicks team. The Chicks decide on a team answer and present it. If they answer correctly, they receive one point and their turn is over. If they answer incorrectly, there is no penalty and their turn is over.

The Dudes answer next. The Chicks team flips to the beginning of the Dudes section of the book and reads the first question to the Dudes team. The Dudes, then, decide on a team answer and present it. Once again, one point is awarded for a correct answer. No points are awarded for an incorrect answer, nor is there a penalty. The turn is simply over.

Each team answers questions read by the opposing team, in the order they are presented in the book. Every seventh question is a Chicks Battle the Dudes Challenge. Knowing when the seventh question arises is easy: there are three questions on every page, 6 on each pair of facing pages. Each time you need to turn the page, you're at lucky number 7!

Chicks Battle the Dudes Challenge

When it's time for a Challenge, the team that is going to answer the question spins the spinner. There are 5 possibilities to spin: *Who Makes Me?*, *Spell It?*, *Finish the Phrase*, *Sex Change* and *Thumb Wrestle*.

If the answering team spins *Who Makes Me?*, *Spell It?*, or *Finish the Phrase*, the opposing team flips to the Challenge section of the book and asks a question from the corresponding category.

a) Who Makes Me? - the opposing team reads the product name listed and the answering team must name the brand or manufacturer listed on the card.

b) Spell It! – the opposing team reads the word listed in quotes as well as the sentence in which it is used, and the answering team must recite the correct spelling of the word.

c) Finish the Phrase – the opposing team reads incomplete phrases from famous movie quotes, song lyrics and advertising jingles and the answering team must fill in the missing words (one blank shown for each missing word) listed on the card.

If the answering team spins Sex Change, they get to answer a question from the opposing team's section of the book. The Chicks get to answer a Dudes question and Dudes get to answer a Chicks question. This should actually be an easier question for your team to answer, so spin and hope for a sex change!

If the answering team spins *Thumb Wrestle*, well, you got it. Each team selects a member to represent them in battle, the two teams count down, 4, 3, 2, 1 - and then it's thumb war.

Teams are awarded two points for answering a Challenge question correctly – even a *Sex Change* question.

Winning the Game

The first team to score 15 points wins!

Chicks

Chicks

 What does the term Jarhead refer to?

 What does feathering refer to in canoeing?

 In baseball, other than the win-loss record, name the statistic that describes a pitcher's performance.

A marine in the United States Marine Corps • Turning the paddle sideways when starting a new stroke • ERA – earned run average

Chicks

 What did the term Flock of Seagulls refer to in 1982?
A. Migrating birds B. A new rock band C. A popular TV show

Name the top-selling American brand of motorcycle.

In baseball, which of the following is not used in determining the Triple Crown Winner?
A. Home runs B. Runs batted in C. On-base percentage

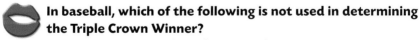

B. A new rock band • Harley-Davidson • C. On-base percentage

Chicks

 Is Philo T. Farnsworth credited with developing the first spinning reel for fishing, canned beer or early television?

 Which of the state quarters pictures a buffalo on the back: Wyoming, Colorado, Kansas or Montana?

 Name the three Cartwright sons on the TV show *Bonanza*.

Early television • Kansas • Little Joe, Hoss and Adam

Chicks

 Besides the elastic waistband, how many elastic straps does an average jock strap have?
A. Two B. Three C. Four

 What flavor of Lifesaver® works best to give off sparks when you bite it in the dark?
A. Wintergreen B. Peppermint C. Spearmint

 What was the name of the first Clint Eastwood Spaghetti Western?
A. *The Good, The Bad and The Ugly* B. *For A Few Dollars More*
C. *A Fistful of Dollars*

A. Two • A. Wintergreen • C. *A Fistful of Dollars*

Chicks

 What is the fastest production car on Earth?
A. McLaren F1 B. Lamborghini Countach C. Porsche Turbo

 Is the largest caliber bullet a .357 Magnum, .44 or 9mm?

 Which of these movies features the F-word the most?
A. *Goodfellas* B. *Scarface* C. *Kill Bill: Vol. I*

A. McLaren F1 • .44 • A. *Goodfellas*

Chicks

 Which boxer said, "Kill the body and the head will die"?
A. Muhammed Ali B. Joe Frazier C. Mike Tyson

 What character in *Animal House* smashed a beer can on his forehead?
A. Bluto B. Flounder C. D-Day

 Female rocker Janis Joplin's version of what Kris Kristofferson song held a spot on the top of the U.S. charts for two weeks in 1971?

B. Joe Frazier • A. Bluto • "Me and Bobby McGee"

 17

Chicks

 What make of guitar was favored by Jimi Hendrix and Eric Clapton?

 What comedian is the co-creator of *Seinfeld* and *Curb Your Enthusiasm*?
A. Larry David B. Jerry Seinfeld C. Jim Burrows

 Which city is the site of the Alamo: Houston, San Antonio or El Paso?

The Fender Stratocaster • A. Larry David • San Antonio

Chicks

 Can you generally lift more weight when doing a curl, bench pressing or moving furniture?

 Should a gridiron be used for clothing, cooking or sport?

 Is a "sheepshank" a bolt, a knot or a metal pen?

Bench pressing • Sport – it's another name for an American football field. • A knot – it is used to shorten rope.

   19

Chicks

 According to Al Pacino in the 1983 film *Scarface*, in what order are power, women and money achieved?

 Is the name of Captain Ahab's ship in *Moby Dick* The Nautilus, The Stars and Stripes or The Pequod?

 In the 1981 film *Stripes*, is Bill Murray in the Army, the Navy or the Marines?

First the money, then the power, then the women • The Pequod • The Army

Chicks

 Which river does not border the island of Manhattan?
A. The East River B. The Bronx River C. The Harlem River

 Which of the following cities is farthest west: Los Angeles, CA, San Diego, CA or Reno, NV?

 In what state was Boys Town, the famous orphanage, founded?
A. New York B. Nebraska C. Oklahoma

Chicks

 What fruit did the British Royal Navy stow aboard ships in order to prevent scurvy among sailors?

 Who is the prayer-saying pro wrestler who held the WWF World Heavyweight Championship from 1984-88?

 Name three members of The Rat Pack.

Chicks

 What is the highest rank attainable in the Boy Scouts?

 Which Civil War general captured Atlanta and led "The March to the Sea"?
A. Robert E. Lee   B. William T. Sherman   C. Stonewall Jackson

 Name the 1970s fantasy role-playing game that utilizes a 20-sided die.

Eagle Scout • B. William T. Sherman • Dungeons & Dragons

Chicks

 In what city does the most popular horse race in the US take place?

 What was the name of Rocky's opponent in *Rocky I* and *Rocky II*?

 Which Wild West outlaw shot a man for snoring loudly: Billy the Kid, John Wesley Hardin or Johnny Ringo?

Louisville – it's the Kentucky Derby. • Apollo Creed • John Wesley Hardin

Chicks

 When the Boston Red Sox won the World Series in 2004, what team did they defeat?

 Would you be more likely to fish for muskie in Minnesota, Missouri or Maine?

 What famous lawman fought the Clantons at the OK Corral?
A. Wyatt Earp   B. Marshall Dillon   C. Wild Bill Hickock

The St. Louis Cardinals • Minnesota • A. Wyatt Earp

Chicks

 Where would you be if you were in Hell's Kitchen?
A. Martha Stewart's house B. New York City C. A Boston restaurant

 In what state can you find Dolphins, Devil Rays and Marlins?

 In *Duck Soup*, what was the name of Groucho Marx's character?
A. Rufus T. Firefly B. Prof. Wagstaff C. Captain Spalding

B. New York City • Florida – these are names of its football and baseball teams. •
A. Rufus T. Firefly

Chicks

 Is a "figure four leglock" a police restraint, a hunting trap or a professional wrestling hold?

 Who was the first man on the moon?
A. Buzz Aldrin B. Neil Armstrong C. John Glenn

 Is the "Spruce Goose" a wild pheasant, an airplane or a lewd groping?

A professional wrestling hold • B. Neil Armstrong • An airplane

Chicks

 Was Cassius Clay a Roman senator, a famous geologist or a boxer?

 In the early 1980s, who brought the band Haircut 100 to national attention?
A. *Rolling Stone*   B. Casey Kasem's Top 100   C. MTV

 In the film *Cool Hand Luke*, Luke won a bet by consuming 50 of what food in an hour?

Boxer - he changed his name to Muhammad Ali. • C. MTV • Hard-boiled eggs

Chicks

 In hockey, what is a "hat trick"?

 Does the 1979 film *Meatballs* take place in an Italian restaurant, at a summer camp or in space?

 Is a "palm cancer" a fatal tumor, a school prank or a tree disease?

Three goals by one player in a single game • At a summer camp • A school prank

   29

Chicks

 Is a "pugilist" a dog-breeder, a boxer or a bond trader?

 In the 1979 film _Breaking Away_, what sporting event or sport is the centerpiece of the plot?

 To what part of the body is a "twack" traditionally applied?
A. The head B. The thigh C. The earlobe

Chicks

What university's sports teams are known as the Hoyas?
A. Howard University B. Georgetown University C. University of Hawaii

What does the slang term "badonkadonk" refer to?

What are the three elements of baseball's Triple Crown?

B. Georgetown University • Large buttocks • Home runs, batting average and RBIs (runs batted in)

Chicks

 Who is a *Playboy* model and the original hostess of MTV's television program *Singled Out*?

 Is the company that produced the Hungry-Man® frozen TV dinner Swanson, General Foods or Kitteredge?

 In *Animal House*, were Otter and Boone frat brothers at Delta House, Phi Sigma Nu or Beta Phi Delta?

Jenny McCarthy (hosted *Singled Out* from 1995-1997) • Swanson • Delta House

 What country is Jean Claude van Damme from?
A. The Netherlands B. France C. Belgium

 What is the traditional drink at the Kentucky Derby: the Mai Tai, Hurricane, Shandy or Mint Julep?

 What was Marvin Hagler's nickname?

C. Belgium • Mint Julep • Marvelous

Chicks

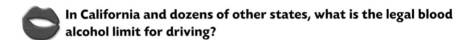

In California and dozens of other states, what is the legal blood alcohol limit for driving?

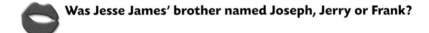

Was Jesse James' brother named Joseph, Jerry or Frank?

Name the most famous Brazilian soccer player in history.

 Chicks

 Name the two New York football teams that don't play any of their games in New York.

 What are waitresses at Hooters called?

 On March 25, 1971, what NFL team changed its name to the New England Patriots?

The Jets and the Giants • Hooters' Girls • The Boston Patriots

Chicks

 Who said, "Damn the torpedoes, full speed ahead!": Lord Nelson, Admiral David Farragut or Stephen Austin?

 What baseball stadium is noted for its ivy-covered outfield wall?
A. Fenway Park B. Yankee Stadium C. Wrigley Field

 What TV show opened with, "...a man barely alive. Gentlemen, we can rebuild him. We have the technology."?

Admiral David Farragut • C. Wrigley Field • *The Six Million Dollar Man*

Chicks

 In what sport would you most likely replace a 'divot'?

 Name the actress who played CJ Parker on the beach-based show *Baywatch*.
A. Carmen Electra B. Pamela Anderson C. Gina Nolan

 What golfer, known for his crazy lifestyle on and off the links, was nicknamed Wild Thing?

Chicks

 Was surfing originally developed in California, Hawaii, Australia or Bali?

 According to a survey of 100 men, in strip poker which would most men take off first: shoes, shirt or pants?

 If you wanted to see the Fighting Irish, would you go to South Bend, to an Irish pub or to Dublin?

Chicks

 Which of the following is not a hat?
A. ranchero B. Stetson C. fedora

 Does Wendy's®, Burger King® or McDonald's® encourage its customers to "Have it your way"?

 Which of the following is not an Elvis Presley movie: *Clambake*, *Kissin' Cousins* or *Viva Tijuana!*?

Chicks

 Which university's sports teams are known as the Demon Deacons?
A. Duke B. DePaul C. Wake Forest

 What state is home to the mountain that is the site of the world's highest recorded land-measured wind speed?

 If you caught a Sockeye, Chinook and Humpback, what species of fish would you have?

C. Wake Forest • New Hampshire (Mt. Washington, 231 mph) • Salmon

  40

Chicks

 In 1980, the US Olympic Hockey Team defeated what country in the "Miracle On Ice"?

 What is a "plumber's helper"?

 What form of petroleum gas is commonly used to fuel outdoor barbeques?

The Soviet Union • A toilet plunger • Propane

 # Chicks

 What two sports are in the winter Olympics' biathlon: bicycling/skating, skiing/riflery or luge/ski jumping?

 On whose behalf are Jake and Elwood Blues on a mission?
A. Their Mother B. BB King C. God

 What is the last name of the three brothers in *Slap Shot*?

Chicks

 Is the distance between bases on a baseball field 40, 60 or 90 feet?

 Which came first: Yahoo!®, Google™ or eBay®?

 When tying a necktie, is it more traditional to use a Windsor, clove hitch or square knot?

90 feet • Yahoo! • Windsor

 43

 Name the sheepish football team that moved from Los Angeles to St. Louis.

 Where will the 2008 summer Olympics be held?

 What model and make of car did Wayne Campbell drive in the movie _Wayne's World_?

The Rams • Beijing, China • AMC Pacer.

Chicks

 Which one of the following actors never starred in an Alfred Hitchcock film?
A. Clark Gable B. Sean Connery C. Cary Grant

 What kind of liquor is Old Overholt?
A. Gin B. Rye C. Vodka

 Where did the world's most powerful recorded earthquake occur?
A. Chile B. China C. California

A. Clark Gable • B. Rye • A. Chile

Chicks

 Which golf club is typically the shortest?

 Does the Colorado River, Rio Grande River or Missouri River create the Grand Canyon?

 Does the typical sauce for baby back ribs have more sugar or salt?

The putter • The Colorado River • Sugar

Chicks

 Did Pittsburgh teams win both the World Series and the Super Bowl in 1979, 1989 or 1999?

 Did Archie Bunker live in Queens, Brooklyn or the South Side?

 Where was the original Playboy Mansion located: Los Angeles, CA, Chicago, IL, New York, NY or Miami, FL?

1979 • Queens • Chicago, IL

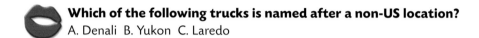

Which of the following trucks is named after a non-US location?
A. Denali B. Yukon C. Laredo

Is a "Melvin" a frontal wedgie, a knee to the thigh or a push into a row of lockers?

Is a "Mountie" a pornographic actor, a plate of mashed potatoes in the UK or a Canadian police officer?

Chicks

 What does a Gimlet cocktail contain?
A. Vodka and tonic B. Gin and soda C. Gin and lime juice

 Name the actor who has portrayed a Bruce Lee opponent, a Vietnam POW rescuer and a Texas Ranger.

 What gourmet dish is prepared with raw ground beef, onions and a raw egg?

C. Gin and lime juice • Chuck Norris • Steak tartare

 What is the official youth magazine of the Boy Scouts of America?
A. *Highlights* B. *Boy's Life* C. *Creem*

 The caber toss, a traditional Scottish athletic event, involves throwing what object?

 The family from *The Sopranos* lives in which US state: New York, New Jersey or Florida?

B. *Boy's Life* • A long, wooden pole • New Jersey

 What annual racecar event takes place each year in the hometown of the Pacers and the Colts?

 What is the last name of the family in *National Lampoon's Vacation*?

 Where do the Super Friends meet?

Chicks

 What masked man called his horse Tornado?

 Would a man be more likely to wear a cummerbund to a wedding, to church or to a rock concert?

 Who is the alter ego of Peter Parker?

Zorro • To a wedding – it goes with a tuxedo. • Spiderman

Chicks

 Which formerly independent Wisconsin brewery brewed Old Style Beer, Special Export and Blatz?

 Spock is half human and half what other race?

 Who was the founder of the magazine *Penthouse*: Larry Flynt, Bob Guccione or Hugh Hefner?

Chicks

 Who is the winningest NASCAR driver of all time?
A. Dale Earnhardt B. Richard Petty C. Jeff Gordon

 What mysterious number is printed beneath the company's motto on every bottle of Rolling Rock beer?
A. 17 B. 33 C. 101

 What is the name of Luke and Bo's cousin in *The Dukes of Hazzard*?

Chicks

 Which is a method for converting iron into steel: the Bessemer process, vulcanization or the Kelvin procedure?

 Who is Luke Skywalker's father?
A. Yoda B. Obi-Wan Kenobi C. Darth Vader

 Why are there dimples on a golf ball?

The Bessemer process • C. Darth Vader • Gives it lift, making it fly longer

Chicks

 Is Rocky Balboa from Chicago, Philadelphia or New York?

 Which college football team did President Gerald Ford, as a student, lead to two undefeated seasons?
A. Ohio State B. Alabama C. Michigan

 What is the name of Britain's overseas espionage bureau?
A. MI6 B. BOEB C. KGB

Philadelphia • C. Michigan • A. MI6

Chicks

 What company developed the Walkman personal stereo?
A. Apple B. Motorola C. Sony

 What Army special forces unit, focused on counter-terrorism, does the Pentagon deny exists?
A. Delta Force B. Green Berets C. NICS

 Name the New York City policeman who in 1971 publicly testified against systematic police corruption and payoffs.

C. Sony • A. Delta Force • Frank Serpico

Chicks

 Which boxer did Robert DeNiro portray in *Raging Bull*: Jerry Quarry, Jake LaMotta or Jack Dempsey?

 In which video arcade game do players drive a car that has machine guns, oil slicks, smoke screens and missiles?
A. Grand Theft Auto   B. Spy Hunter   C. Mission Impossible

 Who is the manufacturer of the SL-1200 MK2 turntable (aka "the 1200"), highly utilized among DJs for decades?

Jake LaMotta • B. Spy Hunter • Technics

Chicks

 How many NBA finals games must a team win to become champion?

 Name the three most popular bar games in America.

 In horseshoes, is a ringer worth three, four or five points?

Four • Pool, darts and liar's dice • Three

Chicks

 Who is the host of TV's *Blind Date*: Jeff Probst, Roger Lodge or Hugh Jember?

 Was the 2005 Super Bowl won by Philadelphia, New England or Indianapolis?

 Are you more likely to find an intake manifold valve in a car, air conditioner, airplane or gas heater?

Chicks

 Which NFL head coach has lead 3 different teams to the playoffs: Mike Holmgren, Tony Dungy or Dick Vermeil?

 Name the West Coast city that voted to outlaw handguns in a 2005 special election.

 Who was the G-man who hunted down Chicago's Al Capone?

Dick Vermeil • San Francisco • Eliot Ness

 What actor starred in the 1968 film *Planet of the Apes*: Sean Connery, Peter Fonda or Charlton Heston?

 What is the name of the computer onboard the spaceship in the film *2001*?
A. Lisa B. AT 2600 C. HAL 9000

 What does a caddie do?

Chicks

 Which US President had the initials USG?

 What is America's October Classic?

 What school did Archie and his friends attend?

 Chicks

 What was the name of the movie star stuck on *Gilligan's Island*?

 If someone in a bar told you to put a "liplock on a longneck," what would they be referring to?

 Which of the following athletes did not attend Stanford University: John McEnroe, Tiger Woods or Steve Carlton?

Ginger Grant (Her first name is good enough) • Taking a swallow of beer – a bottle of beer is a longneck. • Steve Carlton

Chicks

Are "Aussie Rules" an Australian form of football, a style of lovemaking or an Olympic slogan?

Which sport was invented in Ireland: curling, hurling or boxing?

Is West Point (the US Military Academy) located in New York, Maryland, Colorado or Washington, D.C.?

An Australian form of football • Hurling • New York

Chicks

 What are the four strokes in a four-stroke engine?

 Mako, Boston Whaler and Chris-Craft are all makes of what type of vehicle?

 What is the name of the protagonist in J.D. Salinger's *The Catcher in the Rye*?

Intake, compression, ignition and exhaust • Motorboat • Holden Caulfield

Chicks

 Name the documentary filmmaker who made *The Civil War*, *Baseball* and *Jazz*.

 Name the two *Washington Post* journalists who exposed the Nixon administration's involvement in Watergate.

 In *Star Trek*, what type of crystal is used to power the warp drives of the Starship Enterprise?

Ken Burns • Bob Woodward and Carl Bernstein • Dilithium crystals

Chicks

 What beer slogan is "Tastes great, less filling"?

 What poker hand is known as the Dead Man's Hand?

 To bowl 300, a perfect score, how many consecutive strikes are required?

  **Chicks**

 Was it Frank Zappa, Pink Floyd or Led Zepplin who released the album *Sheik Yerbooti*?

 Where can you find two blue lines and a penalty box?

 In the movie *Four Brothers*, directed by John Singleton, name 2 of the 4 actors who play the Four brothers.

Frank Zappa • A hockey rink • Mark Wahlberg, Tyrese Gibson, Andre Benjamin, Garett Hedlund

Chicks

 True or false: The main difference between a traditional lager and a real ale is that lager is bottom fermented and ale is top fermented.

 What is the name of the device that measures how many miles your car has traveled?

 Of Sam Adams, Samuel Smith, Watneys and Fosters, which is the American beer?

 True • Odometer • Sam Adams

Chicks

 Which of the following was the first boxer to defeat Mike Tyson: Robin Givens, Buster Douglas or Michael Spinks?

 Name the only grandfather-grandson combination to become President of the US.

 What two states might we visit while entering and leaving Yellowstone Park?

Chicks

 Where on a canoe are the thwarts?

 Which of *Charlie's Angels* was played by Cheryl Ladd?

 Of Eisenhower, Jackson, Grant and Cleveland, which was not a general?

Kris Munroe • Grover Cleveland

• They are the bars that separate the compartment and run between the gunnels of the boat

 Which is not a character in *Star Trek: The Next Generation*: Captain Kirk, Counselor Troi or Mr. Worf?

 When Mr. Pibb was introduced, what soft drink was it trying to copy: Jolt®, Dr. Pepper®, root beer or Moxie®?

 What city was the home of the Washington Nationals prior to 2005?

Captain Kirk • Dr. Pepper • Montreal, Canada

Chicks

 Is a sousaphone a phonograph, a musical instrument or a radar device?

 In which sport will you find a wicket?
A. Water polo B. Cricket C. Billiards

 Was it Isaac Hayes, Curtis Mayfield or Marvin Gaye who recorded the soundtrack for the 1972 film *Superfly*?

A musical instrument • B. Cricket • Curtis Mayfield

 74

Chicks

 What is the name of Barney & Betty Rubble's adopted son in *The Flintstones*?

 Name the 1980s TV show featuring cocaine-ring-busting cops "Sonny" Crockett and "Rico" Tubbs.

 The cult documentary *Heavy Metal Parking Lot* takes place in an arena lot prior to what band's concert?
A. Metallica B. Iron Maiden C. Judas Priest

Bamm-Bamm • *Miami Vice* • C. Judas Priest

Chicks

 What is the voltage of a home-based electrical outlet in the United States: 90V, 110V or 120V?

 On what planet was Superman born?

 Tonic water, which contains quinine, wards off what disease: hepatitis, polio or malaria?

120V • Krypton • Malaria

Chicks

Who was He-Man's arch nemesis?
A. Skeletor B. The Gremlin C. The Riddler

Name the nerd's fraternity in *Revenge of the Nerds*.

Who was the Texas rock/blues guitarist who died in a plane crash in 1990?
A. Buddy Holly B. Stevie Ray Vaughn C. Ray Charles

A. Skeletor • Lambda Lambda Lambda • B. Stevie Ray Vaughn

 For which American football team did Joe Montana, Jerry Rice and Ronnie Lott play?

 Name the Grateful Dead keyboardist who died early in the band's career.

 Who was on the cover of the first issue of *Playboy*?

Chicks

 Of pine, cherry and walnut, which wood is the softest?

 Name the sport where it is legal to shoot an eagle.

 Other than water, what liquid fills the radiator of a car?

Pine • Golf – it means two under par. • Anti-freeze

Chicks

 In which 1987 movie does Kiefer Sutherland play a vampire named David?

 If I am holding a niblick in my hand, what am I holding?

 Name two of the ingredients used to make gunpowder.

The Lost Boys • A golf club • Sulfur, saltpeter and charcoal (any two of these)

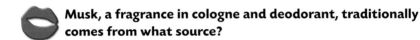

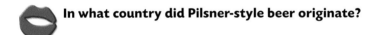 Musk, a fragrance in cologne and deodorant, traditionally comes from what source?

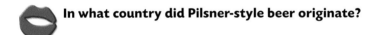 In what country did Pilsner-style beer originate?

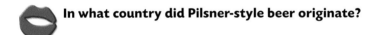 As of 2006, does Barry Bonds, Mark McGwire or Babe Ruth hold the single season home run record?

Barry Bonds (He hit 73 home runs in 2001.)
• Bohemia in the Czech Republic • The testicles of the musk deer

Chicks

 What is a lug nut?

 Is the white foam at the top of a beer called the body, the head, the cream or the gusto?

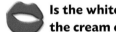 **What country would you be in if you were drinking Asahi, eating tekka maki and watching sumo wrestling?**

The nut that holds a wheel on a car • The head • Japan

Chicks

 In the *Lara Croft: Tomb Raider* series of video games, comic books and movies, what is Lara Croft's royal title?

 Is the National Baseball Hall of Fame and Museum in Cleveland, OH, Springfield, MA or Cooperstown, NY?

 Is the FBI Academy located in Annapolis, Quantico, Chicago or Colorado Springs?

Countess of Abbingdon • Cooperstown, NY • Quantico

Chicks

 Which of the following is not a brand of baseball cards?
A. Fleer B. Topps C. DC

 What actor portrayed Clubber Lang, Rocky's opponent in *Rocky III*?
A. Carl Weathers B. Dolph Lundgren C. Mr. T

 In baseball, if a pitcher throws a perfect game, does he face 24, 27 or 30 batters?

Chicks

What does the term "straight-4" refer to?
A. A poker hand B. A car engine C. A spare attempt in bowling

What brand of deodorant soap has been making men "Clean as a Whistle" since 1972?

True or false: In the US Army, a major outranks a colonel.

B. A car engine • Irish Spring® • False

Chicks

 When dressing for football practice, where did Jack put his cup?

 What branch of the armed forces is represented in *Top Gun*?

 What is the name of the country club in *Caddyshack*?
A. Meadowbrook Country Club B. Westwood Country Club
C. Bushwood Country Club

In his jock strap • The Navy • C. Bushwood Country Club

Chicks

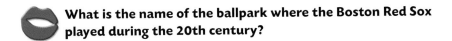
What is the name of the ballpark where the Boston Red Sox played during the 20th century?

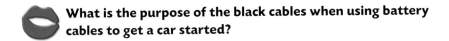
What is the purpose of the black cables when using battery cables to get a car started?

What is so special about the Gillette Mach 3 razor blade?

Fenway Park • To ground the charges or put a negative charge to the battery • It has three razor blades

Chicks

 Clark Kent (aka Superman) is a reporter for what newspaper?

 Name the country star that gave up his seat on the flight that killed Buddy Holly and "The Big Bopper."

 Name the science fiction writer who wrote *Neuromancer*, and is credited as the father of the cyberpunk movement.

Chicks

Name the drummer of Metallica.
A. James Hetfield B. Kirk Hammett C. Lars Ulrich

Who is Elin Nordgren married to?
A. Nomar Garciaparra B. Tiger Woods C. Antonio Banderas

Is a "blue flame" an insult on a porn site's bulletin board, the exhaust burst from a motocross bike or a lit fart?

C. Lars Ulrich • B. Tiger Woods • A lit fart

Chicks

 In *Blade Runner*, does Harrison Ford's character stop an assassination attempt, giant ants or replicants?

 In mammals, which chromosome determines male gender?

 In which sport will you find a scrum: cricket, rugby, soccer or hockey?

Replicants • The Y chromosome • Rugby

Chicks

Where did the St. Valentine's Day Massacre, the famous mafia assassination, take place?
A. Chicago B. Boston C. New York

Which was never a Major League baseball team: The Boston Braves, The Kansas City Athletics or The St. Louis Blues?

What were beer cans originally made of?
A. Tin B. Aluminum C. Steel

A. Chicago • The St. Louis Blues • C. Steel

Chicks

 What was the "Operation" code name for Germany's invasion of the Soviet Union in WWII?
A. Barbarossa B. Overlord C. Condor

 Name the only major championship in men's golf that is played on the same course every year.

 What is the name of the long-standing Los Angeles street gang identified by the color blue?
A. The Crips B. The Bloods C. The Ghouls

A. Barbarossa • The Masters (at Augusta National Golf Club) • A. The Crips

 Was John Wayne's birth name Marion Morrison, Leslie Towne or Roy Wilson?

 The movie *Field of Dreams* took place in what US state: Nebraska, Idaho or Iowa?

 Who is Howard Stern's longtime female sidekick?

Chicks

The classic 1982 guidebook to masculine culture was titled *Real Men Don't Eat* ____.

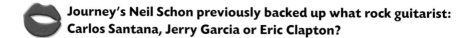
Journey's Neil Schon previously backed up what rock guitarist: Carlos Santana, Jerry Garcia or Eric Clapton?

Name the live concert venue where Johnny Cash recorded "A Boy Named Sue."

 Chicks

 Who won the 2005 World Series?

 What 1970s film featured the song "Singing in the Rain"?

 In the *Fantastic Four* comic books and movie, what ability does the character Reed Richards, Mr. Fantastic, have?

The Chicago White Sox • *Clockwork Orange* • Mr. Fantastic can stretch his body

Chicks

 Who said, "A woman is only a woman but a good cigar is a smoke"?
A. Hugh Hefner B. Groucho Marx C. Rudyard Kipling

 What is a stud finder?
A. A 21st century matchmaker B. A device to find 2x4s behind walls
C. A tool to repair a bicycle wheel

 How many Division I teams are entered into the NCAA Men's College Basketball Tournament?
A. 65 B. 64 C. 128

C. Rudyard Kipling • B. A device to find 2x4's behind walls • A. 65

Chicks

 In what state starting with an "O" would you most likely look for steelhead?

 Was the "Beer That Made Milwaukee Famous" Pabst Blue Ribbon, Schlitz, Miller High Life or Leinenkugel?

 Which of these men is not a college football coach?
A. Mike Krzyzewski B. Larry Coker C. Charlie Weis

Oregon – it's a fish. • Schlitz. • A. Mike Krzyzewski!

Chicks

Is "needle nose" a type of bird, pliers or hose attachment?

What does the acronym "tip" mean?

In woodworking terms, what is a rabbet?

Pliers • To insure prompt service or promptness • A recess or groove cut into the edge of a piece of wood

Chicks

 When fermenting yeast to brew beer, what are the two main by-products?

 In Australia, what are men referring to when they say, "I just spent time with a Sheila"?
A. A beer B. A woman C. A friend's wife or girlfriend

 In what country are you camping if you are in Quetico?

Alcohol and carbon dioxide • B. A woman • Canada

What does the acronym POSH stand for?
A. Port Out, Starboard Home   B. Please Offer Service Homestyle
C. People Ordering Star Hospitality

Name four of the Three Stooges.

Name the sport where participants often "shoot from the paint."

A. Port Out, Starboard Home • Larry, Curley, Moe, Shemp, Joe and Curley Joe • Basketball

 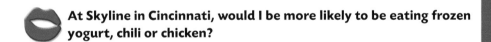 

Chicks

 Why might a man take the herb saw palmetto?

At Skyline in Cincinnati, would I be more likely to be eating frozen yogurt, chili or chicken?

Was Nevada's legendary Mustang Ranch a classic car dealership, a legal brothel or a family dude ranch?

To decrease or maintain the size of his prostate • Chili • A legal brothel

Chicks

battle the

Dudes

Challenge

Chicks battle the Dudes Challenge

Who Makes Me?
Wheaties®

Spell It!
" separate "
Having separate bathrooms can preserve marital harmony.

Finish the Phrase
"Marriage is punishment for _____ in some countries." (Garth in *Wayne's World*)

 # Chicks *battle the* Dudes Challenge

 Who Makes Me?
Speed Stick® deodorant

 Spell It!
" irresistible "
Sandy found Joe's dimples *irresistible*; he finds them embarrassing.

 Finish the Phrase
"The best part of _____ __, is Folger's in your cup." (Folger's coffee)

Colgate • *irresistible* • waking up

Chicks battle the Dudes Challenge

Who Makes Me?
M&Ms®

Spell It!
" harass "
Jenny finds it annoying that she has to *harass* her husband to take out the trash.

Finish the Phrase
"I feel the need... the need for _____!" (Maverick and Goose in *Top Gun*)

 # Chicks battle the Dudes Challenge

 Who Makes Me?
Pine-Sol®

 Spell It!
" indispensable "
Though Colin thinks duct tape is *indispensable*, Heather thought using it to fix the hole in the shower curtain was a little much.

 Finish the Phrase
"Please allow me to introduce myself / I'm a man of ____ __ ____."
("Sympathy for the Devil," Rolling Stones)

Clorox • *indispensable* • wealth and taste

Chicks battle the Dudes Challenge

Who Makes Me?
Scion

Spell It!
" desperate "
Derek was *desperate* to find a last minute anniversary present.

Finish the Phrase
"Have you ever danced with the devil in the pale _____?" (The Joker in *Batman*)

Toyota • *desperate* • moonlight

Chicks battle the Dudes Challenge

 Who Makes Me?
Doritos®

 Spell It!
" occasion "
Hannah has the right outfit for every *occasion*.

 Finish the Phrase
"From the land of sky blue ____." (Hamm's Beer)

Frito Lay • *occasion* • waters

 109

Chicks *battle the* Dudes
Challenge

Who Makes Me?
iPod

Spell It!
" occurrence "
Grace found it a strange *occurrence* that John did his household chores without needing to be reminded.

Finish the Phrase
"I'm the ghost with the ____, babe." (Betelgeuse in *Beetlejuice*)

Apple • *occurrence* • most

Chicks *battle* the **Dudes** **Challenge**

Who Makes Me?
Beanie Babies®

Spell It!
" dissipate "
David finds that gifts of chocolate and flowers can successfully *dissipate* any tension in his love life.

Finish the Phrase
"If I go there will be trouble / An' if I stay it will be _____." ("Should I Stay or Should I Go," The Clash)

Ty • *dissipate* • double

 111

Chicks *battle* the Dudes Challenge

Who Makes Me?
Head and Shoulders®

Spell It!
" accommodate "
During his mother's visits, Mark is challenged to *accommodate* the contradictory wishes of her and his wife.

Finish the Phrase
"We'll always have ____." (Rick Blaine in *Casablanca*)

Chicks battle the Dudes
Challenge

 Who Makes Me?
Pop-Tarts®

 Spell It!
"embarrassment"
Emily blushed with *embarrassment* after tripping in her new heels.

 Finish the Phrase
"They'rrrre ____!" (Frosted Flakes)

Kellogg's • *embarrassment* • great

Chicks *battle the* Dudes Challenge

Who Makes Me?
Liquid-Plumr®

Spell It!
" ecstasy "
Colleen was glowing with *ecstasy* after purchasing two new pairs of shoes.

Finish the Phrase
"Nobody puts Baby in a _____." (Johnny Castle in *Dirty Dancing*)

Clorox • *ecstasy* • corner

Chicks battle the Dudes Challenge

Who Makes Me?
David Beckham's sunglasses

Spell It!
" irritable "
Steve was *irritable* because he had to miss the football game for a dinner party.

Finish the Phrase
"We gotta get out of this place / If it's the ____ ____ we ever do."
("We Gotta Get Out of This Place," The Animals)

Police • *irritable* • last thing

 115

Chicks *battle the* Dudes Challenge

Who Makes Me?
Wonka® candy

Spell It!
" accidentally "
Matt *accidentally* burned himself because he didn't know where the potholders were in the kitchen.

Finish the Phrase
"I've been _____." (Dr. Peter Venkman in *Ghostbusters*)

Chicks battle the Dudes Challenge

 Who Makes Me?
Michelob®

 Spell It!
" broccoli "
Growing up, Max hated his Mom's *broccoli* casserole.

 Finish the Phrase
"Sometimes you feel like a ___. Sometimes you don't." (Almond Joy/Mounds)

Anheuser-Busch • *broccoli* • nut

Chicks *battle the* Dudes
Challenge

Who Makes Me?
Rogaine®

Spell It!
" insistent "
Henry was *insistent* that no one else touch his new grill.

Finish the Phrase
"I always say a kiss on the hand might feel very good, but a diamond _____ lasts forever." (Lorelei in *Gentlemen Prefer Blondes*)

Chicks *battle the* Dudes Challenge

Who Makes Me?
Kingsford® Charcoal

Spell It!
" parallel "
With Ada's help, Ben finally learned to set the pieces of silverware *parallel* to each other.

Finish the Phrase
"I'm just another heart in need of rescue / Waiting on love's _____ _____."
("Here I Go Again," Whitesnake)

Chicks battle the Dudes Challenge

Who Makes Me?
Prius

Spell It!
" criticizes "
Nancy no longer *criticizes* how Richard mows the lawn after trying to do it herself.

Finish the Phrase
"Keep your friends close, but your ___ ___ ." (Michael Corleone in *The Godfather: Part II*)

Chicks *battle the* Dudes Challenge

Who Makes Me?
Ben & Jerry's® Chunky Monkey® ice cream

Spell It!
" absence "
When Janet took the girls on a weekend trip, Rob found the *absence* of females deafening.

Finish the Phrase
"Kiss a little longer with ___ ___."

Chicks *battle the* Dudes Challenge

Who Makes Me?
Swiffer®

Spell It!
" unnecessary "
Harry thinks it's *unnecessary* to have as many jars and tubes of cosmetics as his girlfriend does.

Finish the Phrase
"It's not the men in your life that counts, it's the ___ __ ___ __."
(Tira, played by Mae West, in *I'm No Angel*)

Chicks *battle the* Dudes Challenge

Who Makes Me?
Mach3 razor

Spell It!
" exuberance "
Kirk expressed his *exuberance* after finding the long-lost remote control.

Finish the Phrase
"There is no pain, you are receding / A distant ship's smoke on the _____."
("Comfortably Numb," Pink Floyd)

Gillette® (Procter & Gamble) • *exuberance* • horizon

   123

Chicks *battle the* Dudes
Challenge

Who Makes Me?
212 perfume

Spell It!
" maneuver "
Michael had to *maneuver* in the crowd to reach the attractive girl.

Finish the Phrase
"You had me at _____." (Dorothy Boyd in *Jerry Maguire*)

Chicks *battle the* Dudes Challenge

Who Makes Me?
Herbal Essences®

Spell It!
" heinous "
Josh has a *heinous* sense of fashion, frequently combining plaid with stripes.

Finish the Phrase
"Everybody doesn't like something, but nobody doesn't like ___ ___."

Clairol® (Procter and Gamble) • *heinous* • Sara Lee

125

Chicks *battle the* Dudes Challenge

Who Makes Me?
Rolls Royce

Spell It!
" nuisance "
Chris finds remembering to put the toilet seat down a *nuisance*.

Finish the Phrase
"Better to be a king for a night than a _____ for a lifetime." (Rupert Pupkin in *The King of Comedy*)

Chicks *battle the* Dudes Challenge

 Who Makes Me?
Dockers®

 Spell It!
" rhythm "
Bill was terrified for the wedding dance; he knew he had no sense of *rhythm*.

 Finish the Phrase
"There's a lady who's sure/ all that _____ is gold/ and she's buying a stairway to heaven." ("Stairway to Heaven,"Led Zeppelin)

Chicks *battle the* Dudes
Challenge

Who Makes Me?
Reese's® Peanut Butter Cups®

Spell It!
" seize "
Upon receipt of the time share ad, Nick and Sarah decided to *seize* the opportunity for a vacation.

Finish the Phrase
"I need him like the axe needs the _____." (Jean Harrington in *The Lady Eve*)

Chicks *battle the* Dudes
Challenge

Who Makes Me?
Twinkies®

Spell It!
" privilege "
Hailey and Ethan flipped a coin for the *privilege* of doing the dishes.

Finish the Phrase
"You can't handle the ____!" (Col. Nathan Jessep in *A Few Good Men*)

Hostess® • *privilege* • truth

129

 # Chicks battle the Dudes Challenge

Who Makes Me?
Poison perfume

Spell It!
" noticeable "
Abby pointed out that Connor had a *noticeable* piece of salad stuck in his teeth.

Finish the Phrase
"There's no _____ in baseball!" (Jimmy Dugan in *A League of their Own*)

Dior • *noticeable* • crying

Chicks *battle the* Dudes Challenge

 Who Makes Me?
Land Rover

 Spell It!
" mischievous "
Ashley's *mischievous* grin meant she'd been shopping.

 Finish the Phrase
"How can you just leave me standing? Alone in a world that's so ____?"
("When Doves Cry," Prince)

Chicks *battle the* Dudes Challenge

Who Makes Me?
Charmin®

Spell It!
" nauseous "
Sean gets *nauseous* when his girlfriend drives his Jeep.

Finish the Phrase
"Fat, drunk and _____ is no way to go through life, son." (Dean Wormer in *Animal House*)

Procter & Gamble • *nauseous* • stupid

 132

Chicks *battle the* Dudes
Challenge

Who Makes Me?
The pizza in *Wayne's World*

Spell It!
" presumptuous "
Sam thought it *presumptuous* that Mia would RSVP for him before asking.

Finish the Phrase
"Mr. Clean is the man, behind that _____ – is it wet or is it dry?"

Chicks *battle the* Dudes Challenge

 Who Makes Me?
Colorforms®

 Spell It!
" vacuum "
Ella hates to *vacuum* up all Max's pretzel crumbs.

 Finish the Phrase
"I gave her my heart and she gave me a ___." (Lloyd Dobler in *Say Anything*)

Chicks *battle the* Dudes Challenge

Who Makes Me?
The Jaguar in *Die Another Day*

Spell It!
" realization "
Alex came to the *realization* that things were not going to work out with Alyssa.

Finish the Phrase
"Rows and flows of angel hair / and ___ _____ castles in the air" ("Both Sides Now," Joni Mitchell)

Chicks *battle the* Dudes
Challenge

Who Makes Me?
Michael Jordan's basketball shoes

Spell It!
" permissible "
Flirting with other people was not *permissible* in their relationship.

Finish the Phrase
"Do, or do not. There is no ___." (Yoda in *Star Wars V: The Empire Strikes Back*)

Chicks *battle the* Dudes
Challenge

Who Makes Me?
The condoms in *40-Year-Old Virgin*

Spell It!
" liaison "
The dangerous *liaison* that Myrna had with her boss made her feel guilty.

Finish the Phrase
"How many _____ does it take to get to the tootsie roll center of a Tootsie Pop?"

Magnum • *liaison* • licks

Chicks _battle the_ Dudes Challenge

Who Makes Me?
Frisbee®

Spell It!
" desiccate "
The passion in their relationship began to _desiccate_ after moving in together.

Finish the Phrase
"To infinity and _____." (Buzz Lightyear in _Toy Story_)

Chicks battle the Dudes Challenge

Who Makes Me?
Samba shoe

Spell It!
" drunkenness "
Jeff's *drunkenness* was tolerated as long as he didn't try to kiss the college coeds.

Finish the Phrase
"You are the dancing queen/ young and sweet/ only _____."
("Dancing Queen," Abba)

Adidas® • *drunkenness* • seventeen

Chicks battle the Dudes Challenge

Who Makes Me?
Lamborghini Murciélago from *Batman Begins*

Spell It!
" irascible "
George is undoubtedly an *irascible*, dirty old man.

Finish the Phrase
"I'm not bad. I'm just _____ that way." (Jessica Rabbit, *Who Framed Roger Rabbit*)

Volkswagen • *irascible* • drawn

Chicks *battle the* Dudes Challenge

Who Makes Me?
Snickers®

Spell It!
" misogynist "
Claire felt the reason she didn't get the promotion was that her boss was a *misogynist*.

Finish the Phrase
"Noxema – ___ it all off."

Mars® • *misogynist* • take

  141

Chicks *battle the* Dudes
Challenge

Who Makes Me?
Sprite®

Spell It!
" euphemisms "
Sally was a prude and always spoke in *euphemisms*.

Finish the Phrase
"Waiter, there is too much _____ on my paprikash." (Sally Albright, in *When Harry Met Sally*)

Chicks *battle the* Dudes Challenge

 Who Makes Me?
The volleyball in *Cast Away*

 Spell It!
" cemetery "
On Halloween, everyone gathers at the *cemetery* for a ghoulish time.

 Finish the Phrase
"Layla, you've got me on my _____." ("Layla," Derek And The Dominos)

Wilson® • cemetery • knees

 143

Dudes

Dudes

 Is the name of the main character in *My Fair Lady* Eliza Doolittle, Marni Nixon or Elizabeth Andrews?

 Which legendary actors play the lead roles in 1976's *Robin and Marian*?

 Is "American Girl" a hit for The Guess Who, Tom Petty and the Heartbreakers or Bruce Springsteen?

Eliza Doolittle • Sean Connery and Audrey Hepburn • Tom Petty and the Heartbreakers

Dudes

 Is Kathleen Turner's husband in *Peggy Sue got Married* Nicolas Cage, Michael Douglas or Michael J. Fox?

 Name two of the three actresses who frolic about with Jack Nicholson in *The Witches of Eastwick*.

 Which movie features the song "Cool Rider": *Grease, Grease II or School of Rock*?

Nicolas Cage • Cher, Susan Sarandon and Michelle Pfeiffer • *Grease II*

Dudes

 Name the singer whose *Surfacing* album features the song "Adia".

 Name the actor who plays Dr. Ernest Menville in the Goldie Hawn and Meryl Streep film *Death Becomes Her*.

 Is Denise Austin associated with fitness, gardening, mysticism or literature?

Dudes

 What animal does the fabric cashmere come from?

 Which one of these ingredients is *not* found in a mojito cocktail: sugar, mint, lime juice or pineapple?

 How old is a "virgin" rated Marsala wine: one, two, three or five years of age?

Goat • Pineapple • Five years of age

Dudes

 Which female artist performs the hit song "A Thousand Miles": Norah Jones, Vanessa Carlton or Kelly Clarkson?

 On the hit TV series *The Gilmore Girls*, does actress Lauren Graham play the mother or the daughter?

 Which one of these perfumes is *not* made by Chanel: No. 5, Coco, Allure or Romance?

Vanessa Carlton • The mother, Lorelai • Romance (by Ralph Lauren)

Dudes

 Name the female novelist famous for her first novel, *Uncle Tom's Cabin*.

 Sally Ride became the first American woman in space on June 18 of which year: 1973, 1980 or 1983?

 Bessie Coleman became the first African American female pilot when she was awarded her pilot's license in what year: 1921, 1941 or 1961?

Dudes

 Which massage consists of kneading motions and long strokes toward the heart: Korean, Swedish or Shiatsu?

 To cure static cling you should rub your clothing with which of the following:
A. Plastic bag B. Dampened dryer sheet C. Paper towel

 Is the flower narcissus naturally in season in summer, spring, winter or fall?

Dudes

 Who stars in *Two Weeks Notice* with Sandra Bullock?

 Who became GQ magazine's first ever "Woman of the Year" in 2005?

 Which literary character did Lucy Maud Montgomery create?
A. Heidi B. Jo March C. Anne of Green Gables

Hugh Grant • Jennifer Aniston • C. Anne of Green Gables

Dudes

 The word crochet is derived from the Middle French word croc or crochet, meaning:
A. Stitch B. Weave C. Hook

 A form of lingerie, a basque is a combination of bra and which of the following:
A. Panties B. Garter belt C. Girdle

 What is normally put inside a sconce?
A. Whipped cream filling B. Candles or lights C. Loose tea leaves

C. Hook • B. Garter Belt • B. Candles or lights

Dudes

 What color is the infamous Hope Diamond?

 What dating guide got its title from Sex and the City: Hands Off, He's Just Not That Into You or Shoes and Sex?

 In baking, which of these ingredients is used chiefly as a leavening agent: salt, flour, yeast or cornstarch?

Blue • He's Just Not That Into You • Yeast

Dudes

"Art Nouveau" furniture is a style based on the "new art" of Europe from what period: 1775, 1875 or 1975?

Which goes on first?
A. Bronzer B. Foundation C. Blush

What is Barbie's boyfriend's full name?
A. Ken Carson B. Ken Dahl C. Ken Handler

Dudes

 In *Sleepless in Seattle*, who lives in Seattle: Tom Hanks or Meg Ryan?

 In which movie do Shirley MacLaine and Debra Winger play mother and daughter?

 Who directed *The Virgin Suicides*?

Tom Hanks • *Terms of Endearment* • Sofia Coppola

Dudes

 In Gustave Flaubert's novel *Madame Bovary*, what poison kills the title character?

 Finish this quote from Shakespeare's *Romeo and Juliet*: "My bounty is as boundless as the _____."

 True or false: In ballet, a relevé only involves a dancer's hands.

Dudes

 Which soap opera stars Luke and Laura: *General Hospital*, *All My Children* or *Santa Barbara*?

 What type of onion do Chinese restaurants usually use when making onion pancakes?

 Does Patrick Swayze play a character named Sam Wheat in *Dirty Dancing*, *Ghost* or *The Outsiders*?

General Hospital • Scallions • Ghost

Dudes

 Name the four "C's" to keep in mind while diamond shopping.

 What is a vintner?

 Which removes a lipstick stain: petroleum jelly, nail polish remover, vinegar or lemon juice?

Clarity, cut, color and carat • A person who makes wine • Petroleum jelly

Dudes

What is the name of the daughter born to Gwyneth Paltrow and Chris Martin in 2004: Apple, Peach or Strawberry?

What is Priscilla Presley's maiden name?
A. Beaulieu B. Powell C. Strumpf

Was Humphrey Bogart's *Casablanca* character named Rick Blaine, Phillip Marlowe or Sam Spade?

Apple • A. Beaulieu • Rick Blaine

Dudes

 In sewing and embroidery, what do you call a series of looped stitches that form a chain?
A. Chain stitch B. Sequence stitch C. Link stitch

 What concoction do you fill your birdfeeder with to attract hummingbirds?
A. Sugar/water B. Salt/water C. Lemon juice/water

 Which famous designer created the popular Blush fragrance: Isaac Mizrahi, Marc Jacobs or Coco Chanel?

A. Chain stitch • A. Sugar/water • Marc Jacobs

Dudes

 On *Sex and the City*, does actress Kristen Davis play the role of Carrie, Samantha, Miranda or Charlotte?

 Name the popular blonde bombshell actress/singer who launched her own line of edible cosmetics called Dessert.

 Eccentric Egyptian tycoon Mohammed Al Fayed is known world-wide in part for owning what famous British department store?

Charlotte York • Jessica Simpson • Harrods

Dudes

 When should you have intercourse to increase the chance of getting pregnant?
A. The day after a woman ovulates B. Three days after a woman ovulates
C. Within six days before ovulation

 What astrological sign follows Capricorn?
A. Aquarius B. Scorpio C. Gemini

 True or false: There is a perfume named Chanel No. 4.

C. Within six days before ovulation • A. Aquarius • False

Dudes

 Who is Meg Ryan's co-star in *French Kiss*: Kevin Kline, Dennis Quaid or Tim Robbins?

 Which girl group sang "He's So Fine"?
A. The Supremes B. The Marvalettes C. The Chiffons

 Who sang "(If Loving You Is Wrong) I Don't Want To Be Right": Barbara Mandrell, Loretta Lynn or Patsy Cline?

Kevin Kline • C. The Chiffons • Barbara Mandrell

Dudes

 Which TV show from the 1980s, starring Bruce Willis and Cybil Shepherd, features a character named Agnes DiPesto?

 True or false: Kate Moss and Johnny Depp were married.

 To whom did Stedman Graham become engaged in 1992?

Moonlighting • False • Oprah Winfrey

Dudes

 In Beverly Cleary's books, what is Ramona Quimby's big sister's name: Beezus, Quimby or Amelia?

 Complete the title of this Judy Blume book: *Otherwise Known as _____ ___ ____.*

 What is the name of the little girl in E.B. White's *Charlotte's Web*?
A. Fern   B. Iris   C. Lilly

Beezus • *Sheila the Great* • A. Fern

Dudes

 Name two of the three nicknames behind the initials in the hip-hop group TLC.

 What soap opera actress won the grand prize on the 2005 season of TV's *Dancing With The Stars*?

 Name the two brothers in the 80s boy band *New Kids on the Block*.

Tionne "T-Boz", Lisa "Left Eye" and Rozanda "Chilli" • Kelly Monaco
• Jordan and Jonathan Knight

Dudes

 Is freesia a flower, cooking utensil or frozen yogurt?

 What do the letters L.A.M.B. stand for in Gwen Stefani's clothing line?

 Would you find a chignon on a woman's head or on a dessert plate?

A flower • Love Angel Music Baby • On a woman's head

Dudes

 The method of cutting off leaves or branches in order to remove dead foliage or branches is called what?

 A Chelsea Boot is a pull-on style boot, usually with elastics on the side and at what height on a woman's leg: ankle, knee or thigh?

 The female reproductive parts of a flower are referred to as the what?

Pruning • Ankle • Pistil

Dudes

 What famous jewels are on display at the historic Tower of London?

 In *Bridget Jones: The Edge of Reason*, the story picks up with Bridget happily involved with which of these men?
A. Mark Darcy B. Daniel Cleaver C. Joe Fox

 What TV network, attempting to create a new relationship between women and the media, uses the tagline, "OH!"?

The Crown Jewels • A. Mark Darcy • Oxygen

Dudes

 In what movie did Johnny Depp make his debut?
A. *Platoon* B. *A Nightmare on Elm Street* C. *Edward Scissorhands*

 How long can sperm survive in a woman's body?
A. 12 to 24 hours B. 1 to 4 hours C. 5 to 7 days

 When shaving legs, is it best to shave up toward the waist or down toward the feet?
A. Shave up B. Shave down C. It doesn't matter

B. *A Nightmare on Elm Street* • C. 5 to 7 days • A. Shave up

Dudes

 What is the main ingredient in tofu?

 Which actress wrote the book *Postcards from the Edge*?
A. Carrie Fisher B. Jamie Lee Curtis C. Anne Heche

 Beignets are:
A. Pastries B. Strappy shoes C. Hairstyles

Soybeans • A. Carrie Fisher • A. Pastries

Dudes

 Who was married to Larry Fortensky from 1991 to 1996?

 Was John Travolta's character in *Grease* named Vinnie Barbarino, Joe Kinichie or Danny Zuko?

 Which of the following is *not* a Brönte sister?
A. Charlotte B. Esmeralda C. Emily

Elizabeth Taylor • Danny Zuko • B. Esmeralda

Dudes

 Name the 1989 dance-themed movie that stars Phoebe Cates, Bridget Fonda and Annabeth Gish.

A. *The Twist* B. *Tango* C. *Shag*

 Name the boy that Molly Ringwald's character has a crush on in *Sixteen Candles*.

A. Jeff Templin B. Jake Ryan C. Tommy Harlan

 Frances Hodgson Burnett's book *A Little Princess* features a main character named:

A. Tina Dong B. Moira O'Donnell C. Sara Crew

C. *Shag* • B. Jake Ryan • C. Sara Crew

Dudes

 Give the full names of the two main characters in *Gone With The Wind*.

 Name two of the three members of Destiny's Child.

 Before joining the Blackhearts, Joan Jett was a member of what rock band: The Runaways, The Go-Go's or Vixen?

Dudes

 Which book did Daphne Du Maurier write?
A. *Season of Passion* B. *Rebecca* C. *Wanderlust*

 Is the perfume called *Romance* for Women made by Clinique, Ralph Lauren or Revlon?

 What does the French word "eau," as in "eau de parfum," translate to in English?

Dudes

Finish this popular line from the theme song to the Ellen Degeneres Show: "Let's have a little _____ _____ "

What is broomstick lace?
A. Type of seasoning   B. Form of crochet   C. Shoe design

Whitney Houston recorded the Dolly Parton song, "I Will Always Love You" for what movie?

Dudes

 What color was the 6.5-carat diamond given to Jennifer Lopez by Ben Affleck: pink, blue or yellow?

 Introduced to America in 1966, what famous Belgian chocolatier's signature packaging consists of gold ballotins?

 What historic explorer is credited for being the first European to discover cocoa beans and chocolate in 1502?

Pink • Godiva • Christopher Columbus

Dudes

What was the name of Laura Nyro's first album?
A. *New York Tendaberry* B. *Eli and the 13th Confession* C. *More Than a New Discovery*

Who wrote the original novel titled *Bridget Jones's Diary*?
A. Candace Bushnell B. Ellen Fein & Sherrie Schneider C. Helen Fielding

Who is the third *PowerPuff Girl* with Blossom and Buttercup?
A. Bettina B. Bubbles C. Bluebell

C. *More Than a New Discovery* • C. Helen Fielding • B. Bubbles

Dudes

 Who did Edie Brickell marry in 1992: Paul Simon, Dan Akroyd or Eddie Rabbitt?

 What does the "C" in C-section stand for?

 What kind of lettuce is used when making Caesar salad?

Paul Simon • Caesarean • Romaine

 # Dudes

 What liquid, other than water, is used to make chai tea?

 Name the actress who co-wrote the book *Satisfaction: The Art of the Female Orgasm*.

 The book *Chicks with Sticks: It's a Purl Thing* revolves around girls who:
A. Bake together B. Jog together C. Knit together

Milk • Kim Cattrall • C. Knit together

Dudes

 What famous female entertainer penned the children's book *The English Roses*?

 Finish this Kelly Clarkson ballad: "Oh, I can't believe it's happening to me, some people wait a lifetime for a _____ _____ _____."

 To relieve water retention, should you drink lots of water, eat salted foods or stand on your head?

Dudes

 The most visited mall in the US, the Mall of America, is located where?
A. Bloomington, MN   B. Cleveland, OH   C. Clayton, MO

 Halle Berry, Julianne Moore and Jaime King are all spokeswomen for what famous cosmetics company?

 In 2005, Sarah Jessica Parker debuted her own perfume. What self-described title did she dub her new fragrance?
A. Lovely   B. Beautiful   C. Charming

A. Bloomington, MN • Revlon® • A. Lovely

Dudes

 Window shades that stack in softly tailored folds when open and lie flat when lowered, are commonly referred to as:
A. Honeycomb shades B. Roman shades C. Vertical blinds

 In home décor, a sideboard may also be referred to as a: buffet table, bench or chair?

 If you are shopping for a gift designed by David Yurman, what type of item are you looking for?

B. Roman shades • Buffet table • Jewelry

Dudes

 What do you call a large plate that is part of the initial place setting for a formal dinner table?

 Shallots are part of which family of food?

 What form of lingerie is a peignoir: panties, a dressing gown or a bra?

Charger • Onions • Dressing Gown

Dudes

 On which soap opera did Sarah Michelle Gellar appear?
A. *All My Children* B. *Days of Our Lives* C. *General Hospital*

 On which part of your body would Infusium 23 be used?
A. Your hair B. Your skin C. Your hands

 What is Anna Pavlova associated with?
A. Ballet B. Tennis C. Cooking

A. *All My Children* • A. Your hair • A. Ballet

Dudes

 True or false: The art of Feng Shui is German.

 Who wrote *The Mists of Avalon*, a story about the days of King Arthur told from a woman's point of view?

 Which actress was nominated for a Best Actress Oscar® for *The French Lieutenant's Woman*?

False (It's Chinese.) • Marion Zimmer Bradley • Meryl Streep

Dudes

 What is the name of the high school featured in Francine Pascal's book series?
A. Rydell High B. Sweet Valley High C. Hang 'Em High

 Which company makes Luna Bars®, "The Whole Nutrition Bars for Women"?

 Name the author of *The Witching Hour*, which includes a character named Rowan Mayfair.
A. Anne Rice B. Sue Grafton C. JK Rowling

B. Sweet Valley High • Clif Bar, Inc. • A. Anne Rice

Dudes

In addition to triple sec, lime juice and cranberry juice, what alcohol is used to make a Cosmopolitan?

If you are buying products made by OPI, you are buying products for what part of your body?

Finish this line from Gretchen Wilson's hit, "Red Neck Woman": "I'm a redneck woman, I ain't no ____ ____ ____."

Vodka • Your fingernails and toenails • High class broad

Dudes

 Who was the new face of St. John clothing in 2005: Angela Bassett, Halle Berry or Angelina Jolie?

 Which of the following would you most likely find in a Sephora store?
A. Makeup B. Shoes C. Crockery

 L'Occitane beauty products hail from which part of France?

Angelina Jolie • A. Makeup • Provence

Dudes

 Are Aveda products body/skincare products, a brand of shoes or a line of designer handbags?

 As of 2006, how many times has Susan Lucci's character, Erica Kane, been married on the soap *All My Children*?
A. 10 B. 11 C. 12

 What is star anise?
A. Rare jewel B. Type of spice C. Perfume

Body/skincare products • A. 10 • B. A type of spice

Dudes

 What TV network boasts the tagline "Television for Women"?

 On the TV series *The Golden Girls*, does Bea Arthur play the role of Blanche, Dorothy, Rose or Sophia?

 During the process of eyebrow threading, are hairs being removed, added or replaced?

Lifetime® • Dorothy • Removed

Dudes

 Which of these shoes has the highest heel?
A. Espadrille B. Ballerina C. Pump

 Which of these caters to the youngest age group?
A. Girl Scouts B. Brownie Scouts C. Daisy Scouts

 Who is Barbie's cousin?
A. Tutti B. Skipper C. Francie

C. Pump • C. Daisy Scouts • C. Francie

194

Dudes

 What is gnocchi usually made of?

 The initials in the name of cable channel HSN stand for what?

 True or false: Clothing and bedding for a newborn child is called layette.

Dudes

 What is a demitasse?

 Which jazz singer was born Eleanora Fagan?

 True or false: Cary Grant and Marilyn Monroe never made a movie together.

A small espresso cup • Billie Holiday • False (*Monkey Business*)

Dudes

 Which author wrote *The Cat Ate My Gymsuit* and *Can You Sue Your Parents for Malpractice*?
A. Judy Blume B. Danielle Steel C. Paula Danziger

 What famous female chef hosts the Food Network's cooking program *30 Minute Meals*?

 Is Laura Ingalls Wilder's older sister named Mary, Marcie, Maureen or Martha?

C. Paula Danziger • Rachel Ray • Mary

Dudes

 Name the actress from *Desperate Housewives* who was nominated for an Academy Award for her role in the 2005 film *Transamerica*.

 Dooney & _____ are famous for creating fabulous handbags and accessories.

 The three letters in the popular TV shopping network QVC stand for what?

Felicity Huffman • Bourke • Quality, Value and Convenience

 # Dudes

 Name the band responsible for the albums *1200 Curfews* and *All That We Let In*.

 Name the future web-slinging actor who plays Reese Witherspoon's brother in 1998's *Pleasantville*.

 A torchiere is a type of what?

Dudes

 Bijan on Rodeo Drive, considered the world's most expensive store, has customers who spend an average of:
A. $50,000 B. $100,000 C. $250,000

 What is the world's most expensive spice?
A. Paprika B. Thyme C. Saffron

 A round, strainer-like utensil with lots of holes to drain liquid is referred to as a what?

Dudes

 In a "paraffin hand treatment", what is the main substance used to cover the hands: lotion, wax or milk?

 What grooming tool is available in a scissor shape as well as pointed tip and slanted tip, to name a few?

 Which of these is an alternative to waxing to remove body hair: body sugaring, body exfoliating or body salting?

Wax • Tweezers • Body sugaring

 # Dudes

 Who is famous for her sensuous diaries?
A. Frida Kahlo B. Erica Jong C. Anais Nin

 Who said "The core of the problem today is not sexual, but a problem of identity"?
A. Germaine Greer B. Betty Friedan C. Gloria Steinem

 How many blocks is the "Holy Grail of Shopping", better known as Rodeo Drive?
A. Three B. Four C. Five

C. Anais Nin • B. Betty Friedan • A. Three

Dudes

 Would you be more likely to eat zabaglione for breakfast, dinner or dessert?

 Should you use shower gel on your skin, in your hair or to clean the shower?

 Which of the following is not a sea vegetable (seaweed):
A. Wakame B. Nori C. Tamari

Dessert • On your skin • C. Tamari

Dudes

 Which *Friends* actress made her movie debut in the movie *Leprechaun*?
A. Jennifer Aniston B. Courtney Cox C. Lisa Kudrow

 What is the main ingredient in EPO pills?

 Bebe, the name of a popular women's clothing store, is Turkish for woman, fashion or beauty?

A. Jennifer Aniston • Evening primrose oil • Woman

Dudes

 What kind of buttons does Mary Mack have?

 What is the title of Martha Stewart's magazine?

 Which nail polish remover is best to remove nail polish without damaging the acrylic nails: acetone or non-acetone?

Silver • *Living* • Non-Acetone (acetone eats away at the acrylic faster)

Dudes

 What famous actress said, "I'd rather be looked over than overlooked"?

 Which of Liz Taylor's seven husbands did she marry twice?

 Is a brocade fabric woven with metallic threads called lame or tweed?

Mae West • Richard Burton • Lame

Dudes

 True or false: The star fruit is really shaped like a star.

 If you are cooking with a panini grill, what are you making?

 The term "faux pas", as in "fashion faux pas", literally translates into what phrase in English?

Dudes

 In the fashion world, a "bandini" is another form of what type of clothing?

 In *Pretty Woman*, name the Beverly Hills hotel where Julia Roberts and Richard Gere's character find love.

 In cooking, what would you use a tandoor for?
A. To pulverize   B. To bake   C. To whip

Tube Top • Regent Beverly Wilshire Hotel • B. To bake (it is a clay pot.)

Dudes

 Via Spiga, Rieker and Bruno Magli are all types of what?

 UGG, a company known for making luxurious sheepskin footwear, was founded and is based in what country?

 True or false: While shopping at Sephora, you cannot buy shoes.

Shoes • Australia • True (Sephora specializes in fragrances, cosmetics and body/skincare products)

Dudes

 Complete the title of this magazine: _____ Homes and Gardens.

 In ballet, are pliés done standing up or bending over?

 What fruit is cider vinegar usually made from?

Dudes

 How many "t's" are in the word "shiitake"?

 Name the woman who sings the song, "Stay (I Missed You)", which is featured in the movie *Reality Bites*.

 Lush stores sell:
A. Shoes B. Beauty products C. Underwear

One • Lisa Loeb • B. Beauty products

Dudes

 What do you call the small, ornamental dot in the middle of the forehead worn by women of Hindu descent?

 Sharing its name with a popular Carole King album, what do you call a large piece of decorative fabric that hangs on a wall?

 If you are trying to reduce the appearance of cellulite, which massage should you get?
A. Shiatsu B. Effleurage C. Endermologie

Bindi • Tapestry • C. Endermologie

212

Dudes

 Jennifer Love Hewitt, Mandy Moore and Misha Barton have all been spokeswomen for what skin care products?

 Nicole Kidman was paid $3.5 million to appear in a four-minute commercial for what famous perfume?
A. Obsession B. Eternity C. Chanel No. 5

 Which Desperate Housewife married William H. Macy in 1997?

Dudes

 On the television series, *Desperate Housewives*, which actress plays the character Bree Van De Kamp?

 Italian jewelry designer Elsa Peretti creates pieces exclusively for what famous jeweler?
A. Tiffany & Co. B. Van Cleef & Arpels C. Cartier

 What famous shopping area lies between Wilshire and Santa Monica Boulevards in Beverly Hills, CA?

Marcia Cross • A. Tiffany & Co • Rodeo Drive

Dudes

Name the other main character from _Sex and the City_ besides Carrie, Charlotte and Samantha.
A. Amanda B. Melinda C. Miranda

Who wrote _Sex and the Single Girl_ before becoming editor of _Cosmopolitan_ magazine?
A. Gloria Steinham B. Tina Brown C. Helen Gurley Brown

Which of these is not a top brand of crystal?
A. Nambe B. Waterford C. DeBeers

C. Miranda • C. Helen Gurley Brown • C. DeBeers

Dudes

 Which exercise strengthens vaginal muscles?
A. Kegel exercises B. Leg lifts C. Controlled sneezing

 Which Arquette sister stars in *Desperately Seeking Susan*: Patricia or Rosanna?

 What is puttanesca?
A. A sauce B. A race car C. A type of pasta

A. Kegel exercises • Rosanna • A. A sauce

Dudes

 Larissa Fyodorovich is a character from which novel?

 Name the author of *A Wrinkle in Time* and *A Swiftly Tilting Planet*.

 In the novel *Scarlett*, the sequel to *Gone with the Wind*, do Scarlett and Rhett end up together?

Doctor Zhivago • Madeleine L'Engle • Yes

Dudes

 Name the American novelist who wrote the famous novel *Little Women*.

 What is the name of the character Tom Hanks plays in *Sleepless in Seattle*: Sam Baldwin, Joe Fox or Jimmy Dugan?

 Which Canadian Olympic gold medalist became the first woman to play in an NHL game: Kim St. Pierre, Manon Rheaume or Hayley Wickenheiser?

Louisa May Alcott • Sam Baldwin • Manon Rheaume

Dudes

 The All-American Girls Professional Baseball League was a women's league founded in what year?

 In the blockbuster film *Titanic*, what is the name of the necklace Rose is given by her fiancé, Cal?

 A rutabaga is a root vegetable that most resembles what other veggie?

1943 • "The Heart of the Ocean" • Turnip

Dudes

 "Haricot vert" is French for what vegetable?

 Devonshire cream is a thick, buttery cream also known as: cream cheese, clotted cream or Yorkshire pudding?

 What is the first name of Ellen's DJ on *The Ellen DeGeneres Show*?

String Bean ("green string bean" in French) • Clotted cream • Tony

Dudes

 In Disney's *Beauty and the Beast*, what is the name of the lead female character?

 Name the daughter of Paul McCartney who is a famous designer for the likes of Chloe and Gucci.

 Which female country singer released 1990s *Rumor Has It*?

Belle • Stella McCartney • Reba McEntire

Dudes

 On the *Come Away With Me* album, does Norah Jones play piano, harmonica or flute?

 Which Motown girl group recorded "Reflections"?

 Which 1995 animated Disney movie features the voice of Mel Gibson: *The Lion King*, *Pocahontas* or *Mulan*?

Piano • Diana Ross and the Supremes • *Pocahontas*

Dudes

 On *The Ellen DeGeneres Show*, what does Ellen do on every single episode immediately following her monologue?

 What are the first names of the two Banks children in *Mary Poppins*?

 Was a song called "Steve McQueen" released by Ali McGraw, Sheryl Crow or Norah Jones?

Dance • Jane and Michael • Sheryl Crow

Dudes

 When is the proper time to order an aperitif: before, during or after dinner?

 Does the fabric chambray look more like denim, burlap, silk or wool?

 A kitchen tool used to reduce the toughness of meat is called a what?

Before dinner (It is served to stimulate the appetite.) • Denim • A tenderizer

Dudes

 During the1820s Art Noveau era, the chevron pattern consisted of inverted versions of what letter?

 If you are wearing *7 for All Mankind*, are you wearing earrings, jeans or shoes?

 The term "a la carte" is a French term meaning what in English?

Dudes

 True or false: Both male and female humans have gonads.

 What is the name of the princess in *The Princess Bride*?

 What is the name of the *Dawson's Creek* character played by Katie Holmes?

Dudes

 Film director Cameron Crowe is married to what famous female rocker?

 What are the names of Alex P. Keaton's two sisters on *Family Ties*?

 Who became *Spin City*'s new Deputy Mayor when Michael J. Fox left the series: Charlie Sheen, Rob Lowe or Paul Reiser?

Nancy Wilson of Heart • Mallory and Jennifer • Charlie Sheen

Dudes

 True or false: Katharine Hepburn and Spencer Tracy never married.

 What are the first names of the twins in the original version of *The Parent Trap* (1961)?

 What is the first name of the character portrayed by Kelly Ripa on TV's *All My Children*?

True • Susan and Sharon • Hayley

Dudes

 Name the Scott O'Dell novel that features a young girl fending for herself on an island.

 Who plays the character of Shelby in *Steel Magnolias*?

 In which movie does Harrison Ford play Jack Trainer?

Island of the Blue Dolphins • Julia Roberts • *Working Girl*

Dudes

 Which show starred Dana Delaney as Nurse Colleen McMurphy: *China Beach*, *St. Elsewhere* or *Chicago Hope*?

 What type of garment has a kick pleat?

 Complete the title of the first Nancy Drew book: *The _____ of the Old Clock*.
A. *Secret* B. *Mystery* C. *Case*

China Beach • A skirt • A. *Secret*

Dudes

A snapdragon is a type of:
A. Flower B. Bra hook C. Massage technique

In the world of beauty, does AHA stand for: Alpha hydroxy acids, a happy attidude, or androgenous hair additive?

True or false: In Ancient China, large feet were considered a sign of beauty.

A. Flower • Alpha Hydroxy Acids • False (Small feet were. Binding feet was even practiced to stunt growth.)

Dudes

 Puce is a color that is most similar to:
A. Red B. Green C. Blue

 Which TV show features a main character named Sydney Bristow?

 Which of these female singers was not featured on the remake of Patti Labelle's *Lady Marmalade*: Maya, Lil' Kim, Mary J. Blige or Missy Elliott?

A. Red • *Alias* • Mary J. Blige

Dudes

 Pregnant women should *not* stand in front of which kitchen appliance?

 At which point in your life might you receive an Apgar score?
A. Infancy B. Adolescence C. Kindergarten

 What is the English term for crème anglaise?

Microwave ovens • A. Infancy • Custard sauce

Dudes

 If you are shopping for goods through the manufacturer Hunter Douglas, what are you shopping for?

 Which *Beverly Hills 90210* actor appeared in the movie version of *Buffy the Vampire Slayer*?

 What do you call an ornamental, short drapery mounted across the top of a window to conceal structural fixtures?

Window treatments and accessories • Luke Perry • Valance

Dudes

 Which of these does not feature singer/actress Hilary Duff: *Lizzie McGuire*, *Cadet Kelly* or *All That*?

 Provide at least one first name of the mother/daughter team that makes up TV's *Gilmore Girls*.

 Who is Oprah Winfrey's much talked about best friend?

All That • Rory (daughter) or Lorelai (mother) • Gayle King

ABOUT THE AUTHOR

Always ahead of the game, Bob Moog's newest undertaking is truly novel. As a game inventor, his credits include such favorites as 20 Questions® and 30 Second Mysteries®. As the president of University Games, he has propelled the company he founded with his college pal into an international operation that now boasts five divisions and over 350 products. Whether hosting his radio show "Games People Play," advising MBA candidates or inventing games, Bob sees work as serious fun. He now brings his flair for fun and learning to the bookshelf with the Spinner Books line.

Collect Spinner Books!

ISBN:
1-57528-907-5

ISBN:
1-57528-915-6

ISBN:
1-57528-916-4

ISBN:
1-57528-906-7

ISBN:
1-57528-909-1

Find these books and more at AreYouGame.com or your nearest book or toy store.

2030 Harrison Street, San Francisco, CA 94110
1-800-347-4818, www.ugames.com